People of the Bible

The Bible through stories and pictures

Joseph and His Brothers

Copyright © in this format Belitha Press Ltd., 1982

Text copyright © Catherine Storr 1982

Illustrations copyright © Chris Molan 1982

Art Director: Treld Bicknell

First published in the United States of America 1982
by Raintree Publishers Inc.
310 West Wisconsin Avenue, Milwaukee, Wisconsin 53203
in association with Belitha Press Ltd., London.

Conceived, designed and produced by Belitha Press Ltd.,
2 Beresford Terrace, London N5 2DH

ISBN 0-8172-1976-5 (U.S.A.)

Library of Congress Cataloging in Publication Data

Storr, Catherine.
    Joseph and his brothers.

    (People of the Bible)
    Summary: Retells in simple text and illustrations
the Old Testament story of the conflict between Joseph
and his brothers.
    1. Bible stories, English—O.T. Genesis XXXVII, I-L,
26. 2. Joseph (Biblical patriarch)—Juvenile literature.
3. Bible. O.T.—Biography—Juvenile literature.
4. Patriarchs (Bible)—Biography—Juvenile literature.
[I. Joseph (Biblical patriarch) 2. Bible stories—O.T.
Genesis] I. Molan, Christine, ill. II. Title. III. Series.
BS551.2.S75   1982   222.1'109505   82-9087

ISBN 0-8172-1976-5   AACR2

4 5 6 7 8 9 10 11 12 13 14   98 97 96 95 94 93 92 91 90 89 88

Joseph and His Brothers

RETOLD BY CATHERINE STORR
PICTURES BY CHRIS MOLAN

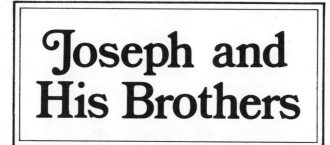

Raintree Childrens Books
Milwaukee
Belitha Press Limited • London

There was once an old man called Jacob. He had several wives and a great many children. He had twelve sons and one daughter. Of all his sons, he loved Joseph the best.

Jacob made Joseph a lovely coat of many colors. He did not give anything to the other boys. This made them angry.

One day, Joseph said to his brothers,
"I had a wonderful dream last night.
I dreamed that we were all out in the fields.
We were binding wheat into sheaves.
Mine was the biggest. All your little sheaves
came and bowed down to mine."

The brothers were furious. "Just because you are our father's favorite," they said, "you think you can lord it over us, don't you?"

The next day Joseph told them another dream. "I was sailing along in the sky, and the sun and moon and eleven stars bowed to me."

Now the brothers really hated Joseph. They agreed they would kill him if they could get him alone, away from home.

Some time later, the brothers were out in the country. They were looking after their father's sheep and goats.

Jacob said to Joseph, "Go out into the country, and find your brothers. Then come back here, and tell me how they are getting on."

When the brothers saw Joseph
coming across the fields,
they said to each other, "Look!
Here comes the great dreamer.
This is our chance to get rid of him.
Let's kill him and throw his body into that
pit."

But the eldest brother, Reuben, did not
agree. He said, "Don't kill him,
just throw him into that pit."
He thought that he would come back later
alone and rescue Joseph.

When Joseph reached his brothers,
they took off his coat of many colors,
and they threw him into the pit.
Reuben was miserable and went away on
his own. The other brothers sat down to
have a meal.

While they were eating, they saw a crowd
of merchants coming along the road.

They had camels loaded with spices, balm and myrrh, which they were going to sell in Egypt.

Then Judah said, "I have an idea!
Instead of killing Joseph,
why don't we sell him?"

So they hauled Joseph up out of the pit
and sold him for twenty pieces of silver.

After the merchants had taken him away,
Reuben came back. He looked into the pit.
Joseph was not there. Reuben thought the
other brothers had killed him.
He was very upset, and said,
"What am I going to tell Jacob, my father?"

Then the brothers killed a goat
and put some blood on Joseph's
coat of many colors.
They took it back to their father, and said,
"We found this coat with blood on it out in
the wild lands. It looks like the coat you
gave Joseph."

Jacob saw that it was Joseph's coat, and
he believed that Joseph was dead. He said,
"An evil beast must have eaten him up.
I shall never see him again."
And Jacob wept for his favorite son.
No one could comfort him.

Jacob did not know that Joseph was alive, in Egypt, and that one day he would see him again.

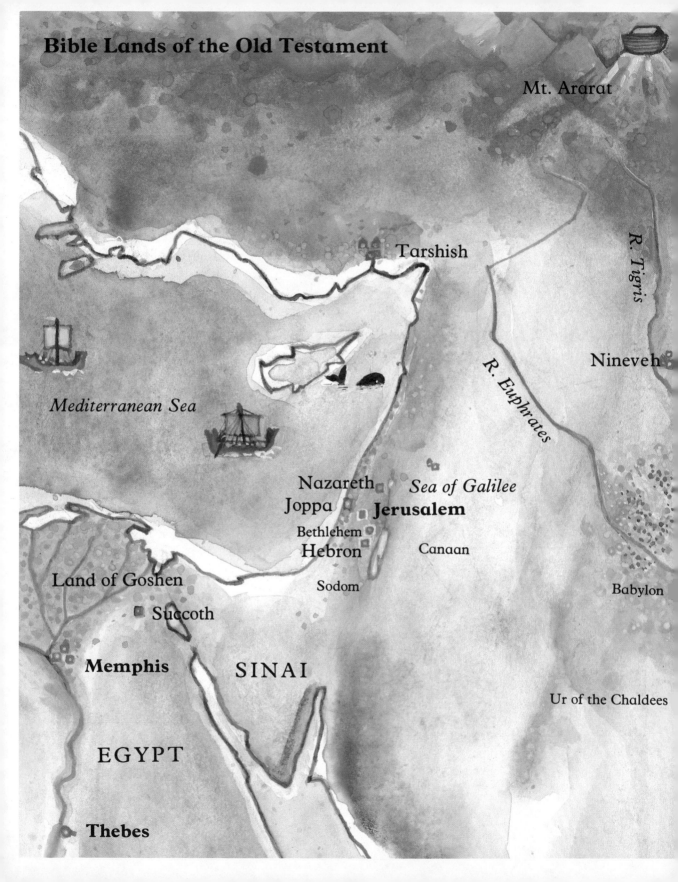

Bible Lands of the Old Testament

Mt. Ararat

R. Tigris

Tarshish

Nineveh

R. Euphrates

Mediterranean Sea

Nazareth

Sea of Galilee

Joppa

Jerusalem

Bethlehem

Hebron

Canaan

Sodom

Babylon

Land of Goshen

Succoth

Ur of the Chaldees

Memphis

SINAI

EGYPT

Thebes